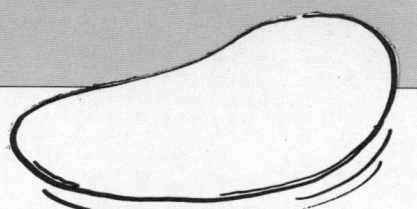

Easter Plus

**Family Activities
from Lent to Pentecost**

Jenny Pate

Collins

Published with the authority
of The Department for Catholic
Education and Formation

People you will meet

Emma has no brothers or sisters. She lives with her mum. She does have some relations - Auntie Joan, Uncle Alex, and cousins Louise and Neil.

Mrs Kelly lives next door. She looks after Emma when she is off school and mum is at work. She lives with Mr Kelly her husband and her two sons, Tom and Dennis. They have a dog called 'Fluff'.

Amina Askari is Emma's friend. She has a sister called Rabaab. They live with their mum and dad.

Moments you will share

Pancake Tuesday	8
Ash Wednesday	10
Fasting and Eating	12
Money Collections	14
British Summertime	16
Mother's Day	18
Reconciliation	20
Palm Sunday	22
Maundy Thursday	24
Good Friday	26
Holy Saturday	28
Easter Sunday	30
Celebrating Easter – Jesus is God's Son	32
Celebrating Easter – Jesus is with us	34
Warmer Weather	36
May Day – Bank Holiday	38
It's still Easter	40
Ascension – Saying Goodbye	42
Pentecost – Birthday of the Church	44
Trinity Sunday	46

Emma sometimes plays with:

Jimmy Greenwood
He is very funny.

Helen Ward
She is great at dancing.

Tommy Roache
He is always the first to have everything.

Using this book

Faith and the Family

Living and sharing faith is a part of family life. Together, parents and children face and respond to life as it comes. By example, and by sharing their values and beliefs they learn from and influence one another. We are all involved in this process. It is not new, neither is it an additional task. As life goes on, so does the process of living and sharing our faith. In the Catholic tradition this is referred to as 'family catechesis': the process of education and nurture in Christian living which takes place in the relationships of everyday life in a family. "Faith is caught, not taught."

However, from time to time we want a more conscious expression of our faith together. We feel a need to pause, collect our thoughts, understanding more deeply the seasons and celebrations that are the framework of family life together.

This is not separate from everyday living, because family interests and concerns are the very stuff of the life and faith we share. The themes that follow are based on some of the highlights and moments a family might share during the seasons of Lent, Easter and Pentecost.

The Liturgical Seasons

Easter

The central, most important feast of the Christian year is Easter. We celebrate the victory of Jesus over sin and death. The suffering and death of the cross gives way to the joy of new life. In celebrating the resurrection we acknowledge that God is with us in the struggles and joys of our own life and death. Because of Easter we are people of hope. Since God is really with us, we have renewed confidence and continue to work to build a better world, the kingdom of God. We undertake to try to bring it about in our own homes, our neighbourhood and the wider world, so far as we can.

Lent

Lent is the special period of preparation for Easter. For adults who wish to be members of the Catholic Church, it is the final stage of their preparation before they are baptised at the Easter Vigil on Holy Saturday night. For those who are already baptised it is one of the Church's key seasons for renewal. In the company of other Christians, we pause, reflect on our lives and our need to change, and draw closer together and closer to God.

For most families Christmas is a time of special celebration of peace and understanding in our homes. It is when memories of Christmas may have faded that the Church begins the season of Lent, a time for turning again to our faith in Jesus who brings into our lives the peace, justice and love of God's kingdom, and a time for renewing our faith that we can live and grow because Jesus is risen and alive.

We begin the season on Ash Wednesday by recognising our sinfulness, our distancing from God and from each other. How can we draw closer? Traditional ways include prayer, fasting and almsgiving.

- Through prayer we consciously place ourselves in the company of Jesus. We need to listen to him if we are to find our way.
- Through fasting we take on the discipline of self-control and learn how hard it is for us to give things up. Fasting helps us to draw closer to God and closer to those who starve and go hungry. Our glimpse into their experience is a way of standing alongside them and it strengthens our resolve to work for a better, fairer distribution of the world's food.
- Through almsgiving we give thanks to God for the many blessings we have received. We try to help others by sharing with them what we have.

Drawing closer together and building a better world is not easy: it brings its own struggles. It is the presence of Jesus and his example in accepting the cross that helps us to face the struggles and difficulties of our lives.

Pentecost

At Pentecost we celebrate the coming of the Holy Spirit. We celebrate the birthday of the Church and are strengthened to play our part in it. The Spirit is gift to each of us. God calls each one of us. The gift of the Spirit is a real sign of God's confidence in each of us as individuals and all of us together as a community. God knows what we have to offer and believes that we can make a difference to the world. The coming of the Spirit renews our confidence in ourselves because God is with us as we work for the kingdom: the world the way God intended it to be.

Moments to share

Allowing for some choice there are sufficient themes to provide one for each week of the season, except Holy Week, when there are suggested materials for Palm Sunday, Maundy Thursday, Good Friday, Holy Saturday and Easter Sunday. Each theme has a story, activities for children, thoughts for adults, suggestions of things to do with the children sometime during the week and a prayer.

Story

The story of Emma and the people in her life may or may not be like that of anyone you know. There is no norm for family life. People who have read Emma's story found it helpful. It is meant to help us move into the theme through our life experiences. Read to or with children, it can act as a trigger to help us reflect and think about our own situation. Some people likened it to a soap opera! It's meant to be enjoyed.

Activities

Each theme has activities aimed at children from about six to eight years old. Depending on their skills and interest, younger and older children may enjoy them too. Whatever their age, the children will need the interest and support of adults or young adults, to help them to do and enjoy the activities. The purpose of these is to deepen the children's understanding of the theme or to follow it up in their own lives. For some the activities may hold more interest than the story and may be used as a substitute.

Thoughts for adults

When working with children many adults find that they have more questions than answers. They too begin to wonder and search for meaning. The 'thoughts' here only touch on some aspects of the theme, they are 'food for thoughts' for adults; not to be shared directly with the children.

With the children

The suggestions are made to start you thinking. They are simple practical ways of living and sharing your faith. Your own ideas will be far more integrated into your own experience and your family's usual routine.

Prayer

The prayers are suggestions only. Each family will have its own way of praying together.

Using the material at home

These are some ideas and suggestions as to how you might use this book.

- The material is intended to be used once a week. Choose whichever day suits you or spread it out over the week. It is important to make it as much a part of your usual routine as you can:
- Read the story whenever you would ordinarily read to or with children.
- Use the activity sheet whenever they show interest or when they are 'bored' and complain that there's nothing to do.
- Use the ideas suggested in 'with the children' whenever appropriate, whenever the opportunity presents itself.
- Use the prayer at a suitable time, for example: bedtime, before or after meals that you have eaten together or after reading the story. Interrupting whatever is happening in the house so that you can gather to pray is perhaps the surest way of making prayer unpopular.
- Have something to look at: an attractive candle on the meal table or by the bed, a favourite light, for example, the light that keeps children

company during the night. Place the Easter Garden, decorations and eggs where the family Christmas tree usually stands.
- Give the children time for private prayer, a few seconds of silence. Let them speak out aloud if they wish. Keep it short and keep them involved.

It is important to pace yourself. The seasons of Lent and Easter through to Pentecost last for almost fourteen weeks! There might be the temptation to hurry through a few themes and activities or to read the story through. If handled this way, many of the opportunities for deepening and understanding the significant moments of the seasons will be lost.

When some of the family are not interested

Not everyone will be interested in all that is suggested. Don't force anyone. Sometimes children, especially older ones, reject the prayer life (including Mass) of their parents even when the example has been good. This can leave parents feeling that the children 'have lost their faith' and that they, as parents, have in some way failed. Many adults find that their husband or wife shows no interest either, leaving the interested partner on their own.

Prayer and worship are a part of our faith life. Holiness is expressed and nurtured in all sorts of ways, often through action, service and good works. In these ways members of the family make a powerful contribution to the whole process of living and sharing faith in a family. The process itself can draw families closer together.

Using the material in other settings

This material is intended for home use by parents, grand-parents, god parents, aunties, uncles, neighbours and friends, etc. With some adaptation it might also be used in the parish by:
- family groups preparing for sacraments;
- parents' groups: Lent groups, mother and toddler groups, playgroups, coffee mornings;
- children's Liturgy of the Word groups as activities to take home;
- family retreats;
- youth clubs, e.g. rainbows, beavers, brownies, cubs etc.

Schools and teachers in search of ideas may also find the suggestions useful.
Finally: **N.B. Adapt, adapt, adapt!**

Pancake Tuesday

'Pancakes, pancakes,' thought Emma as she hurried out of school, 'pancakes, pancakes.'

When Emma reached Mrs Kelly's door she could smell them. Tom, Mrs Kelly's son was standing at the cooker. The pancake he was making was nearly ready.

"Watch this, Emma!" he shouted. Tom tossed the pancake in the air and caught it again.

"I'll get it higher this time," said Tom.

He gave the frying pan a great jerk and out flew the pancake. It hit the ceiling then split in two. Tom caught one half but the other half stuck to the light-fitting. The dog began to bark. He barked so loudly that Mrs Kelly hurried into the kitchen.

"That's it!" she shouted. "I'll do the cooking if you're going to play about."

Tom and Emma kept out of the way and sat quietly while Mrs Kelly took over the cooking. She did make lovely pancakes.

Later on at home mum made pancakes from a packet because she was so tired. While she cooked them she taught Emma a rhyme that she had sung as a little girl:

"Pancake Tuesday is a very happy day,
if we don't get a pancake
we'll all run away.
Where shall we run to?
Down ....(add a local name), Lane.
Ahh! Here comes ....(teacher's name)..
with a big fat cane!

Pancake Recipe

For about 4 pancakes you will need:
50 grams (2 ozs) plain flour   Bowl
1 egg – size 4   Sieve
50ml. (1/4 pint) milk   Fork/ whisk
1/4 teaspoon of salt   Frying pan

Mix
Step 1. Sieve the flour with the salt into the bowl.
Step 2. Make a hole in the centre and put the egg inside.
Step 3. Pour into the middle half of the milk, a little at a time and start to mix from the middle outwards.
Step 4. Beat until the mixture is smooth and bubbly then cover the bowl and leave for half an hour.
Step 5. Beat in the rest of the milk.

Cook
Cover the frying pan with a little fat. Pour in enough mixture to thinly cover the bottom of the pan.
Cook until golden brown on one side, turn and brown the other side.
Add sweet or savoury fillings:

Honey	Sausages
Jam	Bacon
Marmalade	Cheese
Fresh fruit	Mince
Tinned fruit	Chicken
Syrup	Mushrooms
Sugar and lemon	Chutney
Cream and nuts	Tomato sauce

Thoughts for adults

The tradition of eating pancakes on the eve of Ash Wednesday started when there were strict fast rules during Lent. Certain foods were not to be used. Pancakes were ideal for using up the bits of food that otherwise might be wasted. It was the family's way of preparing for the season of Lent.

Though we no longer need to empty the cupboards, making pancakes remains one of our strongest traditions and is kept by people of all ages. The fun and chaos of making, tossing and eating pancakes draws us closer together. This feeling of closeness is something that we continue to work at during Lent. Pancake Tuesday prepares us well.

Such closeness can be hard work and at times requires more from us than we feel we can give. For us, as Christians, the struggle is worthwhile, we know that by drawing closer to each other, we draw closer to God.

A thought from Scripture: Luke 14:12-14.

With the children

- Discuss favourite pancakes, memories of past Pancake Tuesdays.
- Sing the pancake rhyme.
- Teach them how to make pancakes.
- Talk over ways in which you could re-create the family atmosphere at home which is part of the Christmas Season. Lent is another season for Christians to be at their best.

Say a prayer together:

God our Father,
You are the giver of all good things.
Thank you for our pancakes.
Thank you for the fun of making and eating them.
Thank you for the friends and family we ate them with.

Now that Lent is beginning,
please show the ways to make where we live
into a happy, friendly place.
We ask for your help as friends of yours
who want to be closer to you and more like you in every way.
Amen.

Ash Wednesday

Emma was very proud. She had a huge blob of ashes on her forehead; more than anyone else. The other children laughed but she took no notice.

"What's that?" asked Amina her friend. "Ashes," said Emma. "It's a sorry sign and mine's the biggest! I haven't rubbed mine off because I want to show mum. I can't wait. I got more than anyone else".

"May I touch them?" asked Amina. "O.K." said Emma. "Big isn't it?"

Amina touched the ashes and bits fell into Emma's eyes. Emma knocked Amina's arm away hurting her and at the same time rubbed off all her ashes by accident. They began to fight.

When Emma got to Mrs Kelly's her eyes were red and her face was dirty. "Go and get washed before your mum comes," said Mrs Kelly.

Emma wouldn't, she just sat and sulked. She was still very angry.

When Mum arrived she asked Mrs Kelly what was the matter. Mrs Kelly shrugged her shoulders. "She won't tell me."

"You had better change your mood by the time we get home," said mum.

With that Emma stuck her tongue out at mum and Mrs Kelly. They were very shocked! Then Emma cried, said sorry and gave them both a kiss and hug.

"Well," said Mum, "that's the biggest sorry sign we ever had!"

Sorry badges
Here are some ideas for sorry badges to make and give to friends and family

Thoughts for adults

The ceremony of ashes has its roots in the early days of the Church. Those who had committed serious and public sins, such as murder or denying the faith, were given one opportunity to reconcile themselves with the Christian community. The reconciliation ceremony was presided over by the bishop and took place on Maundy Thursday.

The penitents prepared for this over a period of time that might be as long as two or three years. During that time they were given harsh penances to perform. They might, for example, be asked to cover themselves with ashes or wear goatskins. This practice only lasted a few hundred years in the Church, but the symbolic wearing of ashes continues to be a sign of sorrow for our sins and of our desire to seek God's help, in order to rededicate ourselves to living our Christian lives in communion with Jesus. The receiving of ashes on our forehead also reminds us of the fact that we are 'dust', that life will pass and our bodies change and die.

Receiving ashes is also an important part of our lives together as a parish family. We recognise that we need to say sorry to one another. It is by reconciling ourselves to each other that we are reconciled to God and can help to bring about the kingdom of peace.

A thought from Scripture: Joel 2:12-18; Matthew 6:5-6.

With the children

- Discuss the story. Who else did Emma need to say sorry to and why? What would make everyone in the story happier? Do you think anyone else needed to say sorry?
- Have a 'say sorry day'. Say sorry to each other.
- Make and colour some smiley and sorry badges or cards. Choose some people to give them to.

Say a prayer together

Jesus, help us to remember and never forget
that you know it's hard to be good;
and that you love us and forgive us
no matter what we have done.
Help us too, to forgive one another
as you forgive us. Amen.

Fasting and Eating

The children in Emma's road were having a great time playing out together when she was called in for lunch. Amina went in too but only for a moment. Her big sister Rabaab wished she could have gone in but it was Ramadan and only Amina in their family could eat or drink before dark.

Emma looked at her lunch saying, "I don't like sprouts or the potatoes done that way."

"You have eaten them that way before and you ate sprouts off my plate last week. Eat it up," mum replied.

Emma ate everything but the sprouts. She could hear the other children playing and she remembered that there would be no sweets or biscuits after this meal. She had given them up for Lent. She wanted to play outside.

"Can I leave my sprouts?"

"No, they're good for you and I'm not finishing any more of your meals." Mum meant it.

Emma mashed up one sprout and spread it around the plate to pretend that it was eaten. She hid two others under the table and put one in her pocket. She was just about to mash another when Mrs Kelly popped in with the dog, so Emma tried to give the rest to the dog under the table.

Mum caught her and was angry.

"There are starving children who would love that food!"

"They can have it," thought Emma.

Thoughts for adults

We have all faced a time when like Emma we would have gladly sent our lunch halfway around the world to whoever needed it, but we knew it was useless to try. Fasting during Lent can seem equally useless on the face of it; it might appear to help no one. However the experience of anyone who has been on a diet or hasn't been able to buy or eat food for whatever reason, is that their attitude to food changes. Food becomes very precious, their respect for it increases.

Food is precious. We know that people die from the lack of it and whilst eating less may not change the situation, it does give us a tiny insight into the experience of being hungry. This insight may spur us on to work for a more even distribution of the food in the world.

Lent is a good time to review our eating habits. Like dieting, fasting is a discipline which can be difficult. It demands self-denial, self-control and determination. This can be good for us and strengthen us as people. By eating less we can draw closer to the people who starve, keeping them in mind throughout the season rather than just for the length of a news item. By eating less we can save money and give it to those who are hungry.

People of other faiths also recognise the value of fasting. The Muslim practice of Ramadam encourages self-discipline and respect for food. From dawn till dusk nothing is eaten or drunk, including water. Children as young as nine take part. Parents may allow their children to break the fast on one or two days for good reasons. Children younger than nine are encouraged not to eat or drink between meals. When the nine year olds begin the fast for the first time they are given a party and presents on the evening of the first day, as a sign of support. Families usually meet on a Saturday evening to pray, read the Koran and encourage each other. When the time of fasting is over, food or money is given to the poor.

A thought from Scripture: Isaiah 58:7 or Matthew 6:16-18.

With the children

- Talk to each other about food likes and dislikes.
- Tell each other how you feel when you see hungry people on TV.
- Plan a sensible eating day together. Fill out the menu and agree on foods that everyone will enjoy.
- Agree what to do with the savings.

Say a prayer together

Lord Jesus,
we are sorry for throwing food away, while others have none.
We are sorry for throwing away clothes, while others have none.
Please help us not to be greedy, taking more than our fair share.
Please help us not to be lazy, when hungry people need our help.

Money Collections

At last it was Saturday. Emma had been saving up so that when she went to the shops she could buy a poster of her favourite pop star. When she and mum got to the shop they met a lady shaking a collecting tin.

"Let's cross over," said mum. "I'm short of money this week. I may have to borrow from your money box again."

They crossed over and they saw Tommy Roache. His coat was full of stickers saying 'Save the Whale'.

"I bought all these," he said proudly, "from a woman by the Post Office."

"We don't have to go to the Post Office," said mum to Emma before Emma had time to say anything.

They had nearly finished their shopping when they met Tom and Dennis Kelly who were collecting money too. Their tins said: FOR THE HUNGRY.

"We can't pass this one.
Come on Emma, put some of your money in too."

"I haven't got much and
I'm saving up. Can I give some next week?"

"It's now those people
need food," said mum opening her purse.

Emma looked at her
money and looked at mum.

(What do you think
she did next?)

14

Which tin?

Put these coins into the collecting tins by drawing a line between the coin and the tin. *(Strict rule: you can only use each coin once!)*

Thoughts for adults

There are so many demands on our money – street collections, school collections, church collections, TV appeals, etc., that we have to be selective about who we give our money to. The choice is not easy. We often hear it said that 'charity begins at home'; but where is home. Is it our immediate or extended family, our street, neighbourhood, town, country or all the world?

We are fast learning, particularly environmentally, that what happens on one side of the world affects the other side, so too with the economy. Sometimes one nation is richer because another is poorer. We must be concerned as Christians, that everyone has fair shares, each according to their need.

A thought from Scripture: James 2:14-17; or Matthew 6:1-4.

With the children

- Agree which tins will have your money.
- Make a family collection box.
- List all the charities that you know about and agree where to send your family Lent collection.

For prayer time

One day Jesus was talking to his friends and he said:
One of these days I will say,
"When I was hungry, you gave me something to eat.
When I was thirsty, you gave me something to drink.
When I was a stranger, you made me feel at home.
When I was cold, you gave me something warm to wear.
When I was ill, you came to see me."
Then you will say: "When were you hungry, and when did we give you something to eat?
When were you thirsty? When did we give you something to drink?
When were you a stranger? When did we make you feel at home?
When were you cold? When did we give you something warm to wear?
When were you ill? When did we come to see you?"
Then I will say: "If you tried to help anyone at all, you did something for me!"
Taken from **Listen**, A.J. McCallen (*Collins*)

British Summertime

Helen Ward was knocking loudly on the door and it woke Emma up.

"Are you ready?" she asked. "We're off to the baths."

Emma was still in her nightie. She looked over. Tommy, Jim and Amina were all climbing into Mrs Ward's car.

"Sorry Emma, we can't wait, we have to go," shouted Mrs Ward.

The car drove off and Emma ran to wake mum up. When mum woke up she realised that she had forgotten to change the clocks.

"Can I go by myself, I know the way?" pleaded Emma.

"Certainly not, you're too young!" said mum.

Emma went into a sulk and wouldn't eat her breakfast or get dressed.

Next Mrs Kelly arrived very upset because she had had a row with Dennis, her son. He had come in very late and she wasn't pleased.

"He's blaming it on the extra hour," she explained to mum. "I wish they wouldn't mess about with the time."

Mum put the kettle on. "Yes, but I do like the brighter evenings, and now that you're older Emma, you can play out after tea."

Emma started to smile and think about getting dressed.

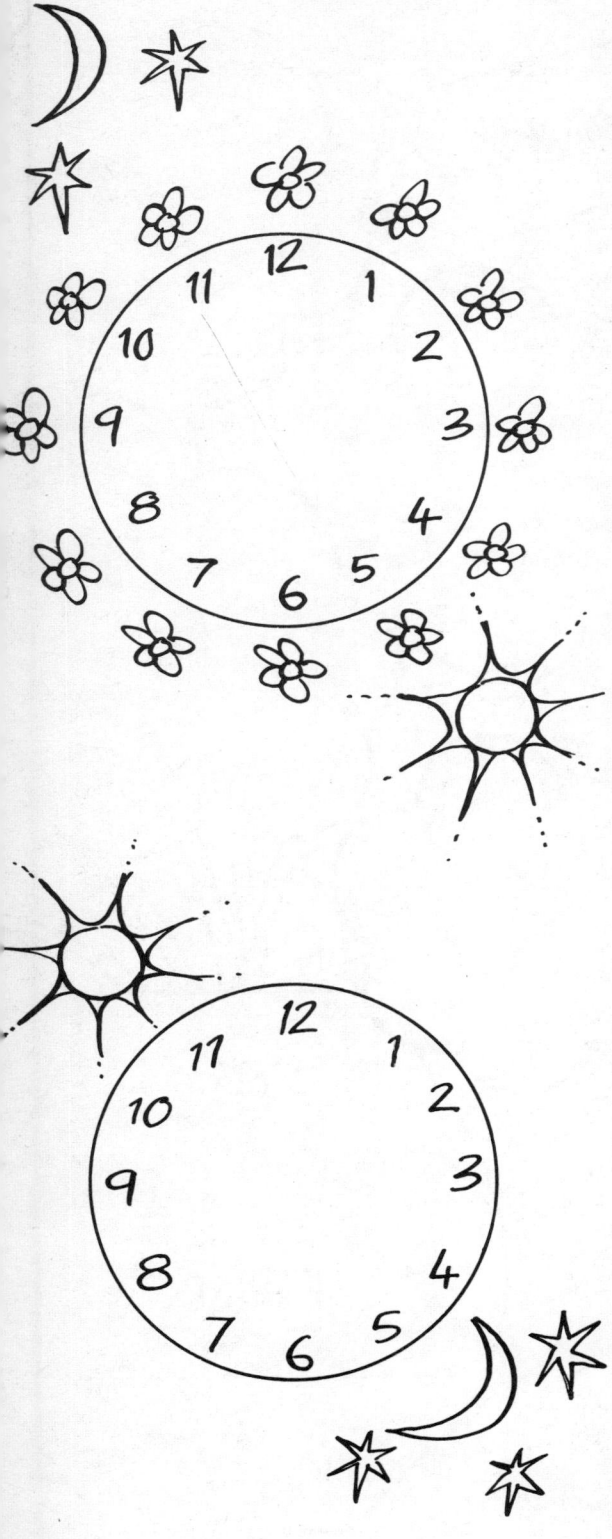

Thoughts for adults

We seem to have no choice, the clocks move on, take us by surprise and throw us into confusion. For a day or two we can feel a little disorientated as we try to recover the hour of lost sleep. The brighter evenings can make it seem worthwhile, though sometimes the weather is so lousy that the benefits seem lost. Nevertheless, it's a sign that Spring and Summer are on their way and life may be a little better. We pay the price of an hour's lost sleep.

The clocks move on in our lives too. Children become argumentative, sulky teenagers struggling for their independence. They can make life difficult, but the difficulties become worthwhile when we see them grow and mature, even though such growth is often slow and disguised. During this time we learn to let go (though part of us dies), and to watch the new life of the young adult emerge.

The clocks move on and the patterns of our lives bring ups and downs: struggle (cross), letting go (death) and new life (resurrection). There are always brighter days ahead!

A thought from Scripture: James 1: 2-4.

With the children

- Talk about and complete the activities together.
- Plant some seeds. Explain that if they are to grow they need to be put into dark wet soil.
- Talk over the things children are struggling with. Help them to see how their struggles may be necessary if they are to move on to better things.
- Fill the house with daffodils.

Say a prayer together

Lord Jesus,
your life was not an easy one.
During these weeks of Lent
may we keep you company.
Help us not to avoid the difficult times,
help us to see that such times can help us to grow
and become better people.
Amen.

Mother's Day

It was the first time Emma had been allowed to go to the shops on her own. She was very proud of herself and very proud of the makeup-bag that she had bought mum and the chocolate bar that she had bought for Mrs Kelly.

On the way home she met Tommy Roache. He was showing off the huge box of chocolates he'd bought for his mum. Suddenly the Kelly's dog got out of the house and ran towards them. Emma quickly lifted up her presents away from Fluff who was jumping up to get them. Emma began to run and fell over. She let out such a scream!

Mum heard her cry. Emma heard mum's footsteps. Emma had cut her head and had to be taken to hospital for stitches.

When they returned home Emma gave mum her present and the card that she had made in school. Mum loved them both, especially the card, even though it opened out on the wrong side.

"How did you know that I had fallen over?" asked Emma.

"I know your cry, you're my little girl," said mum.

"Yes, and I know your footsteps!"

Thank you

Say thank you to mum or whoever looks after you.

Draw or write in each flower something that you are thankful for.

Thoughts for adults

God is love. It is through the loving experiences in our life that we come to know God. A parent's love for a child might not be the finest, but it can give us a glimpse of God's love for us, his/her children.

In the story mum knew Emma's cry. Though she had let her go to the shops on her own, she wasn't far and she was there when Emma needed her. She recognised her cry because she was her own. The footsteps brought Emma comfort, she knew her mother well.

Mother's Day is always celebrated on the 4th Sunday of Lent, in the heart of the season. It's a reminder to us all that God is very close to us as we struggle to draw closer to him/her.

A thought from Scripture: Isaiah 49:14-15.

With the children

- Have some fun together.
- Tell them how much you love their notes, cards (especially upside-down ones!) and presents.
- Tell them that you still love them even when they've misbehaved.
- Explain why you sometimes say 'No' (possible dangers, etc.).
- Fill-out the flowers.

Say a prayer together

God, Jesus taught us to call you Father;
thank you for your love.
Help us to always remember that you are close
when we need you.
Help us to remember that you really do hear our prayers
even if you sometimes say no.
Please help us to put our trust in you
just like your Son, Jesus did.
We are friends of his.

Jesus' Mother was Mary. There is a special prayer which celebrates her love of God and her love for us:
Hail Mary, full of Grace
the Lord is with you.
Blessed are you among women,
and Blessed is the fruit of your womb Jesus.
Holy Mary, Mother of God,
pray for us sinners,
now and at the hour of our death. Amen.

Reconciliation

Emma came in, she had knocked at all her friends' houses and none of them were able to play out. She was surprised and pleased to see Auntie Joan and her cousins Louise and Neil in the sitting room. 'Great,' she thought. 'I can play with them!'

Louise and Neil were keen to see Emma's toys, so she proudly showed them all her best things. They chose the 'walkie talkies' to play with.

It wasn't long before they were fighting. There were three of them and only two 'walkie talkies'.

"Play with something else," called mum.

They looked in the toy box, but everytime Louise or Neil touched one of Emma's things she told them off. It wasn't long before another fight began.

"Come downstairs and watch TV," called mum.

They settled in front of the TV. Emma was glad they were there, she liked company. After a while Neil began to make scarey noises and say scarey things about Emma's house. It wasn't long before the girls screamed and ran to their mothers. Neil was told off.

The doorbell rang and it was Uncle Alex. He had come to take Auntie Joan, Louise and Neil home. As they waved goodbye mum asked Emma, "Would you like a brother or sister to play with?"

Emma said....

What do you think?

At the end of each line put a ✓ for yes or ✗ for no or ? sometimes.

- If someone hits you, hit them back? ... ☐
- 'Finders, keepers, losers, weepers'? ... ☐
- You should lend your toys, etc? .... ☐
- You should borrow people's things? ... ☐
- Your friends should only play with you? ☐
- It isn't naughty to be angry? .... ☐
- After an argument you should make friends even if it wasn't your fault? ...... ☐
- Girls should only play with girls and boys with boys? .... ☐
- It's alright to tell people what you think of them? .... ☐
- You should give everyone a second chance? .... ☐
- You should only play with people your own age? .... ☐
- If it's your ball or bike or toy then you're in charge? .... ☐
- Sometimes it's good to let others choose ☐
- Brothers and sisters must share everything? .... ☐
- It's alright to call people names just for a laugh? .... ☐
- It's fair to do a job at home even when it's not your turn? .... ☐
- The oldest always makes the rules? ... ☐
- Everyone should get a present on your birthday? .... ☐
- Mum and Dad are the only people who can tell you what to do? .... ☐

Thoughts for adults

Relationships are difficult no matter what our age. Quickly broken or spoilt they need time, strength and courage to rebuild. During the season of Lent we particularly try to rebuild our broken relationships with each other and with God. It's not easy.
We can draw strength from Jesus' story of the Prodigal Son:

> The young son, having left home, returns a failure. His reason for coming home is to find food (his reason may sound familiar to many parents). He is greeted by his father with great excitement. His father is thrilled to see him. He asks for no explanation, he is just glad to have his son home.
> The father then plans a party which upsets the elder son who is jealous of the fuss and attention given to his younger brother. (Again, parents may understand the father's point of view; occasionally one child needs extra love, attention, etc. This doesn't mean that the other children aren't loved).
> In spite of the poor relationship between the brothers, the party goes ahead, though we know that the celebration would have been all the better if there had been reconciliation between the brothers.

The Sacrament of Reconciliation is our turning back to God who welcomes us in our imperfect state. Even though we are just as likely to make the same mistakes, he is glad that we have come to him and want to change. We celebrate God's forgiveness, and our celebration of reconciliation with him will be all the richer for our reconciliation with each other.

A thought from Scripture: Luke 15:11-32.

With the children
- Talk about and complete the activity.
- Talk over how arguments begin and can be put right.
- Ask for your child's forgiveness and show your own.

For prayer time

God says this:
Come back to me and be sorry.
Turn back to me for I am gentle
I am slow to lose my temper
and very quick to forgive you
if you have done wrong. (Taken from **Praise**, A.J. McCallen, *Collins*)
(Pause and allow time for each one privately to say sorry to God. Ask for his strength to help you to say sorry to each other.)

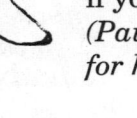

Palm Sunday

Tommy, Helen, Amina, Jim and Emma were staring into the corner shop window choosing Easter eggs. The Easter holidays were coming soon and they were very excited. They were each shouting, "I'm getting that one!" and pointing to an egg.

"I'm also getting new clothes," said Amina, "our fasting time will soon be over and we all have new clothes."

"So am I," said Tommy, "and we're going to our caravan."

"I'll be going to my nan's," said Helen.

"Well, I'm going to play football every day, all day," said Jim. "I want to join the estate football team."

"I'm going to be at home with mum!" said Emma.

The others didn't seem interested in what Emma said, they carried on talking about Easter eggs.

'They don't understand,' thought Emma. 'I love being at Mrs Kelly's, but I love mum being off work even more. I'll have a better time than any of them.'

She went home and looked at the palms behind the crucifix that she and mum had carried home so carefully from church that day. One had been folded into a cross, the other was straight and far larger than the cross it was tucked behind. 'Easter is beginning, Easter is beginning,' thought Emma.

Which egg?

Choose your egg.
Turn to page 48
to find out what is inside.

Thoughts for adults

When Jesus arrived in Jerusalem with his followers to celebrate the passover, many people came to greet him and there grew a great air of excitement. The people who gathered had high expectations of Jesus. Many thought he would lead them in a revolution against the Roman occupation.

Not everyone was pleased to see him. As the excitement grew the Romans became anxious. The welcome Jesus received worried the Jewish religious leaders too. He had challenged their way of doing things so many times that he had become a threat to their authority.

The time had come to celebrate the Passover. For this feast there were a great many customary activities and Jesus and the disciples kept to the traditions in the days leading up to the feast.

A thought from Scripture: Luke 19:47-48.

With the children

- Pick an Easter egg. After they have chosen and discussed what's inside, explain the saying, 'Don't judge a book by its cover'. Talk about how we make the same mistake with people.
- Talk over Easter traditions in your house. What does everyone expect to happen? What might happen this year? What are the restrictions, money, etc?

Say a prayer

Wave your palm and:
"Sing hosanna! Sing hosanna,
Sing hosanna to the King of Kings.
Sing hosanna! Sing hosanna,
Sing hosanna to the King."

Jesus, you are a king
but you don't look like one.
You haven't any fine clothes,
 you haven't even a house,
and you are riding a donkey.
You are a king who takes us by surprise!
Repeat: "Sing hosanna...

Maundy Thursday

The school holidays had begun and mum did have extra time off work though not until after Easter, so Emma stayed with Mrs Kelly for the first few days.

"We're going shopping," said Mrs Kelly. "It's a long holiday and we will need plenty of bread as well as all the extra things for Sunday."

The shopping centre was very busy. There were crowds everywhere.

"It's worse than Christmas," one man moaned.

"Yes," said a lady, "bread is sold out already."

That put Mrs Kelly into a panic. She grabbed Emma and ran to every bread shop in the centre. Whilst Mrs Kelly was in a queue, Emma wandered over to Cohen's, her favourite shop. She was glad it was open; it had been closed for two days earlier that week. She enjoyed the smells that drifted out of the doorway. Pressing her face up to the window she saw a large plate with six insets deep enough to be bowls. It was decorated with a beautiful pattern. Wow!' she thought.

Mr Cohen noticed Emma. "You're Emma. You're in my son Eric's class aren't you?" Emma nodded. "That plate is for Passover, a very special celebration."

"We're having a very, very special Mass in church tonight too," said Emma. "Father Gallagher asked everyone to bring a first Communion photo for the noticeboard, just for tonight."

Then Mrs Kelly arrived with so much shopping she could hardly walk. Emma shared the load. As well as the usual shopping they had to carry the special Easter shopping. Mr Cohen laughed at the two of them.

"Good luck ladies!" he shouted.

When mum arrived at Mrs Kelly's, Emma noticed an Easter egg and a bottle of wine on top of mum's shopping. She looked closer to see what else might be there.

Mrs Kelly's Shopping
Colour red all the special Easter shopping
Colour yellow the ordinary shopping

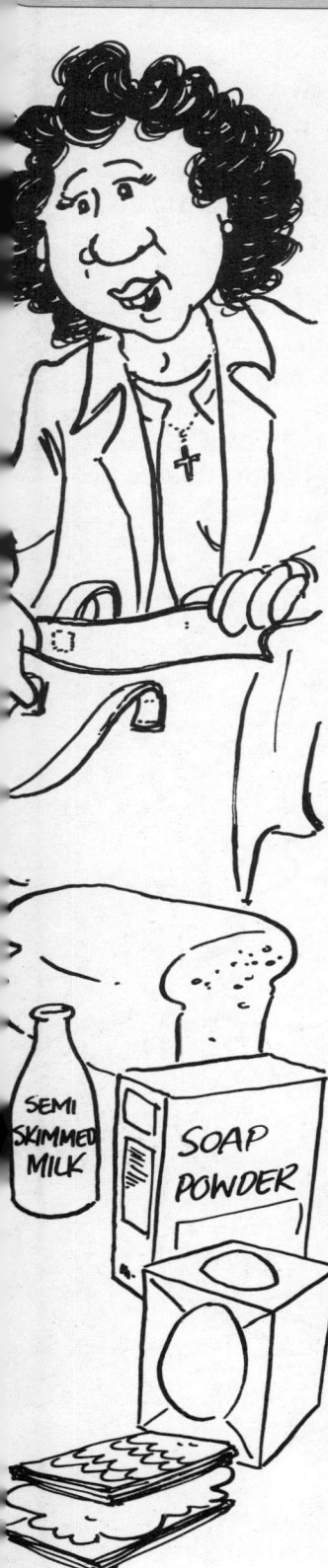

Thoughts for adults

At the Last Supper Jesus took bread from the table; he blessed it and broke it and gave it to his followers saying, "This is my body". Then he took the cup of wine; he blessed it and gave it to them saying, " This is my blood".

Jesus chose bread as a sign of our everyday lives – the ordinary but essential stuff of life – to show that he is with us in everyday events, even when they are broken and crummy: low income, homelessness, broken families.

Jesus chose wine as a sign of the exciting parts of our lives, for wine can cheer us up and help us to celebrate. Jesus wanted us to know that he is with us in these moments too.

At the Last Supper, Jesus was celebrating the Passover Meal with his followers. The Jewish feast of Passover, celebrating freedom from slavery, occurs on the 14th day of the month Nisan (Nisan is approximately April). The feast, like Easter, is movable. Families prepare and celebrate this season (eight days) by, amongst other ways, thoroughly cleaning their homes, fasting and resting from work. An entire set of crockery and cutlery are especially set aside for use during this period. The climax is the Passover Meal which is celebrated at home in family groups.

A thought from Scripture: Luke 22:19-20.

With the children

- Talk about the 'special' and ordinary food amongst your Easter shopping.
- Remember and talk about First Communion celebrations: your own, older children's, something for younger ones to look forward to.
- Talk about going to communion and remind the children that they don't have to be 'good' to go to communion. They go because they need Jesus' help to become better people.

Say a prayer together

Lord Jesus, at your last supper you picked bread to remind us
that you are with us everyday.
Thank you!
You picked wine to remind us
that you are with us in all the special times too.
Thank you!
Lord Jesus,
we want to be with you in communion.
We want to be with you by being close to each other.

Sing or say: Do not be afraid, for I have redeemed you.
I have called you by your name; you are mine.

Good Friday

Mum was busy cleaning the house, there was nothing else for Emma to do but to sit on their front step. The road was empty except for Tommy who was kicking a football and eating an Easter egg. 'I'll have to wait till Sunday for my egg,' thought Emma. Suddenly she heard a noise coming from the end of the road. She ran to see what was happening.

The gang from the other end of the estate had come to tease Amina and start a fight. They were standing around her calling her names and laughing at her.

"Stop it," shouted Emma. "She's my friend, leave her alone!"

Though Emma was very frightened she ran to Amina and took hold of her hand. Jimmy Greenwood was there too, he ran for his dad. When the gang saw Mr Greenwood they ran away.

"Well they aren't as brave as you!" said Mr Greenwood to Amina, Jim and Emma.

Emma and Amina had always been friends, but from that day on they were best friends. Their mums were glad to see them.

An Easter Garden

You will need:
baking tray filled with sand/soil
play dough for shaping into hill
2 egg boxes : one for rock tomb; one planted with cress seeds. (Cress may take 5/6 days to sprout.)
Lolly ice sticks   Palms (or other greenery)

Thoughts for adults

Today is called *Good* Friday even though it is the day on which Jesus died on the cross.

It is *Good* because Jesus on the cross is a sign of God's love for us. In giving his life, rather than fleeing from death, Jesus shows us that love is stronger than death and good is stronger than evil.

When Jesus was raised back to life, God our Father confirmed the truth of all that Jesus said and did. The cross is a sign of the depth of God's love. Jesus' resurrection is a sign of God's victory over evil and death.

Today is *Good* because we know that Jesus gave his life for each one of us. He did so not because we earn his love, but because he gives us his love freely. Now each of us can know how much God loves us.

A thought from Scripture: Isaiah 52: 13- 53:12.

With the children

- Read to them or show the video of *The Lion, the Witch and the Wardrobe* by C.S. Lewis. Aslan the Lion's self-sacrifice for his friends will help give the children an insight into the death of Jesus.
- Begin to prepare your Easter garden.

Say a prayer together

Jesus, you stood by us your friends.
You wanted us to know
how great is God's love for us.

Help us to stand by our friends
and those who need us
so that they too will know God's love.

Help us when we are frightened
and help us to forgive our enemies.
We ask this as friends of yours
who are thinking about you a great deal today.
Amen.

A food tradition

Hot cross buns
Hot cross buns
If you have no daughters
give them to your sons.
One a penny,
two a penny,
Hot cross buns!

Is this song fair?
How many hot cross buns will
you need in your house?

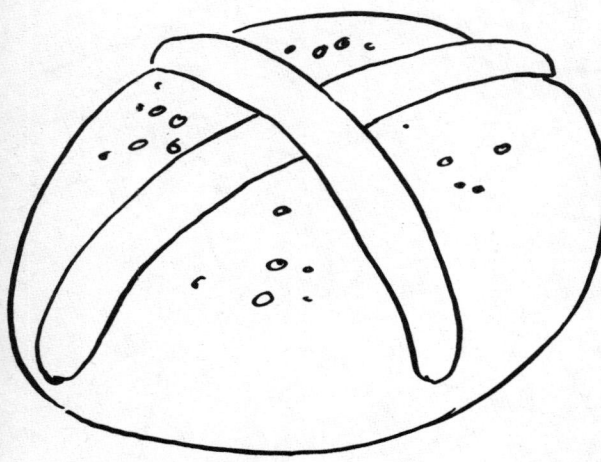

Could you cut this bun into even pieces, enough to give each person in your house a fair share?
Use a pencil to mark the pieces.

Holy Saturday

Cups, saucers, plates, dishes of every kind were scattered over the floor. Emma stepped over them to the fridge. Opening the door she asked, "Can I have some cake?"

"No, it's for tomorrow. Close the door and watch where you put your feet!"

Closing the door, Emma stood on a plate and broke it. "It was an accident, an accident, honest mum!"

"Out, out to play – you're under my feet!"

Emma hurried out into the street but there was no one to play with. Everyone was being kept in after yesterday's trouble. She knocked on Mrs Kelly's door thinking that she'd get her Easter eggs early.

"I'm off to church," Mrs Kelly told Emma as she answered the door. Emma's eyes were fixed on the eggs on top of the cupboard. Mrs Kelly noticed. "Not until tomorrow. Help me carry this clean linen to church. It's all ready now for tomorrow."

The church was full of people cleaning, arranging flowers, putting out boxes of candles. There was even a huge candle being decorated in the middle of the church.

As they walked home Emma gave a big sigh. "I can't wait until tomorrow. The holidays are boring, there's nothing happening."

"Wait and see, you never know what tomorrow brings," said Mrs Kelly.

Around your Easter Garden
Add a Paschal Candle, flowers, eggs and flags.
Here are some designs to start you off.

Thoughts for adults

Unlike the first Easter, Easter Sunday now holds few surprises. Holy Saturday has become a day of anticipation and preparation with many of the events of the next day predictable. However, God cannot be staged by us. Rarely does he act in our lives on cue or quite as we hope and plan. We do not know how things will turn out. We do not know what will happen tomorrow. We must wait and see.

Activities

- Tend your Easter garden - wait for the seeds to grow. Prepare your homes and wait for tomorrow.

With the children

(The Easter Vigil ceremony is the highlight of the Church's year, but it is not wholly suitable for children. Below is a shortened 'at home' version.)
You will need:
A large white candle as the Paschal Candle.   A decorated candle stand.
A sticky label with the year (e.g. 1991)   Candles for all the family.
Holy water.   (If possible a bonfire to light the candle, but matches will do.)

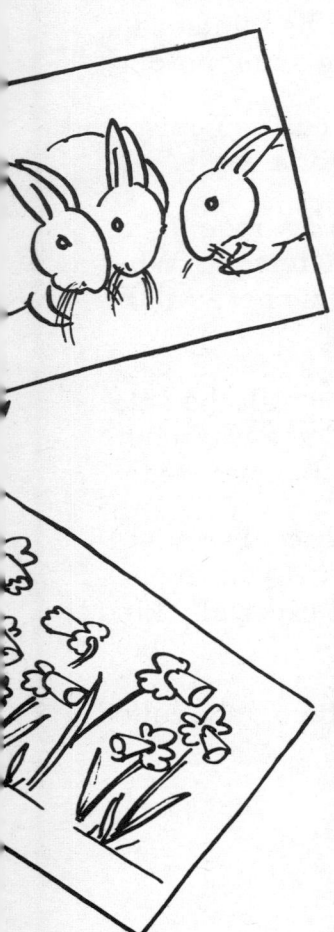

The Celebration begins in a special place. Wait until it is dark, turn off all the lights, gather outside by the bonfire, or by the front door.
Prayer: This is the holiest night of the year. It is the night when Jesus died and came alive again. We celebrate this knowing that one day we too will share this new life with Jesus.
Light the 'Paschal' candle and then write or stick on the current year .
Glory be to Jesus, Yesterday, Today and Tomorrow, from the beginning of time to the end of time. Guard our family and keep us safe. Amen.
Everyone lights a candle from the Paschal Candle. Follow the Paschal candle indoors saying three times. Christ our light: Thanks be to God.
Place the paschal candle on its stand and sing a song of praise.
(The Vigil would continue with the Liturgy of the Word. After the Gospel the baptismal waters are blessed and any adult baptisms would take place. Then all renew their baptismal promises. The children can do. this. Everyone holds their lit candle .)
Q. Do you want to be good? A. **I do.**
Q. Do you believe in God our Father who made all things. A. **I do.**
Q. Do you believe in Jesus his Son whose mother was Mary, who lived, died and came alive again and now lives with God our Father in heave? A. **I do.**
Q. Do you believe in the Holy Spirit who helps us to be good? A. **I do.**

(Put the candles in stands, bless yourselves, give each other a hug and have a party!

Easter Sunday

As soon as she woke Emma remembered that it was Easter Sunday. 'Easter eggs!' she thought. She jumped out of bed, pulled back the curtains, only to see that it was pouring with rain. She was surprised, she thought Easter Sunday would be sunny.

Downstairs on the table was an Easter egg from mum. It was just the one she wanted!

Later on that morning, after church, Mrs Kelly gave her one, so did the Kelly boys.

After lunch when Emma was finishing one of her eggs and mum her wine, the 'phone rang. When mum had finished talking on the 'phone she announced,

"Your Auntie Joan and cousins Louise and Neil are coming to stay for a while."

"Yeah! Can they sleep in my room?" Emma squealed with excitement. 'What a surprise,' she thought. 'Life here will be different now.'

She then pestered mum for all the details. It was exciting news and she wanted to talk about it. After a while mum said,

"Emma, give me some peace, I've a lot to think about. You go and get your room ready! I hope you will be especially kind to them."

"Yes I will, I've missed them," she called as she climbed the stairs.

Thoughts for adults

The news that Jesus was alive took his followers by surprise. The women who were the first to hear it weren't believed; the men said they wanted proof. Later, meeting Jesus for themselves they had their proof. Not everyone recognised Jesus at first. The two disciples returning to Emmaus were so preoccupied with the events of the last few days, they didn't realise that it was Jesus who walked with them. Indeed it wasn't until he broke the bread at their table that they recognised him.

Each of the followers experienced and heard the news of Jesus' resurrection in a different way. Surprised, delighted, confused and bewildered they were all keen to share their experiences with others. They knew too that life could never be the same.

Throughout Lent we have been drawing closer to each other, closer to God. For us too, life cannot be the same. Easter confirms our direction, gives us confidence and hope.

A thought from Scripture: Mark 16:6-7.

With the children

- Add flowers, eggs around the Easter Garden.
- Help the children make Easter cards and write thank you letters.
- Have your own Paschal candle, a large white candle surrounded with flowers (or pot pourri) at the base. Light it at meal times and prayer time.

At prayer time

Remember each family member (and special friends) by name.

Alleluia, alleluia!
God bless.....,
God bless....., etc.
May they be especially happy this Easter.

Jesus, during Lent we tried hard
to share in your sorrow and the sufferings of others;
Now that Easter has come we are especially happy;
help us to share this happiness with others. Amen.

Celebrating Easter – Jesus is God's Son

On the last day of the school holidays mum and Auntie Joan took Emma, Louise and Neil for a day out. Jim Greenwood, who had become a good friend of Neil's, came too. They had a great time.

While they ate their picnic Louise pestered them with questions about everything. She always did this. Neil nicknamed her 'Twenty Questions'.

"Go and play and give us five minutes peace," pleaded Auntie Joan. They ran off to play except for Emma, who wanted to stay with mum and Auntie Joan.

"She's a shy girl, just like me," said mum.

"Yes she has her grandmother's gentleness too, unlike Louise. She's outgoing, dashes into everything like her father. She doesn't miss a trick either. Neil has our Joe's sense of humour. He often reminds me of him," said Auntie Joan.

"Young Jim there is so like his mother too," said mum. Emma looked at Jim, he did look like his mum and he sounded like her too. 'They are alike,' she thought, 'and they like doing the same things.'

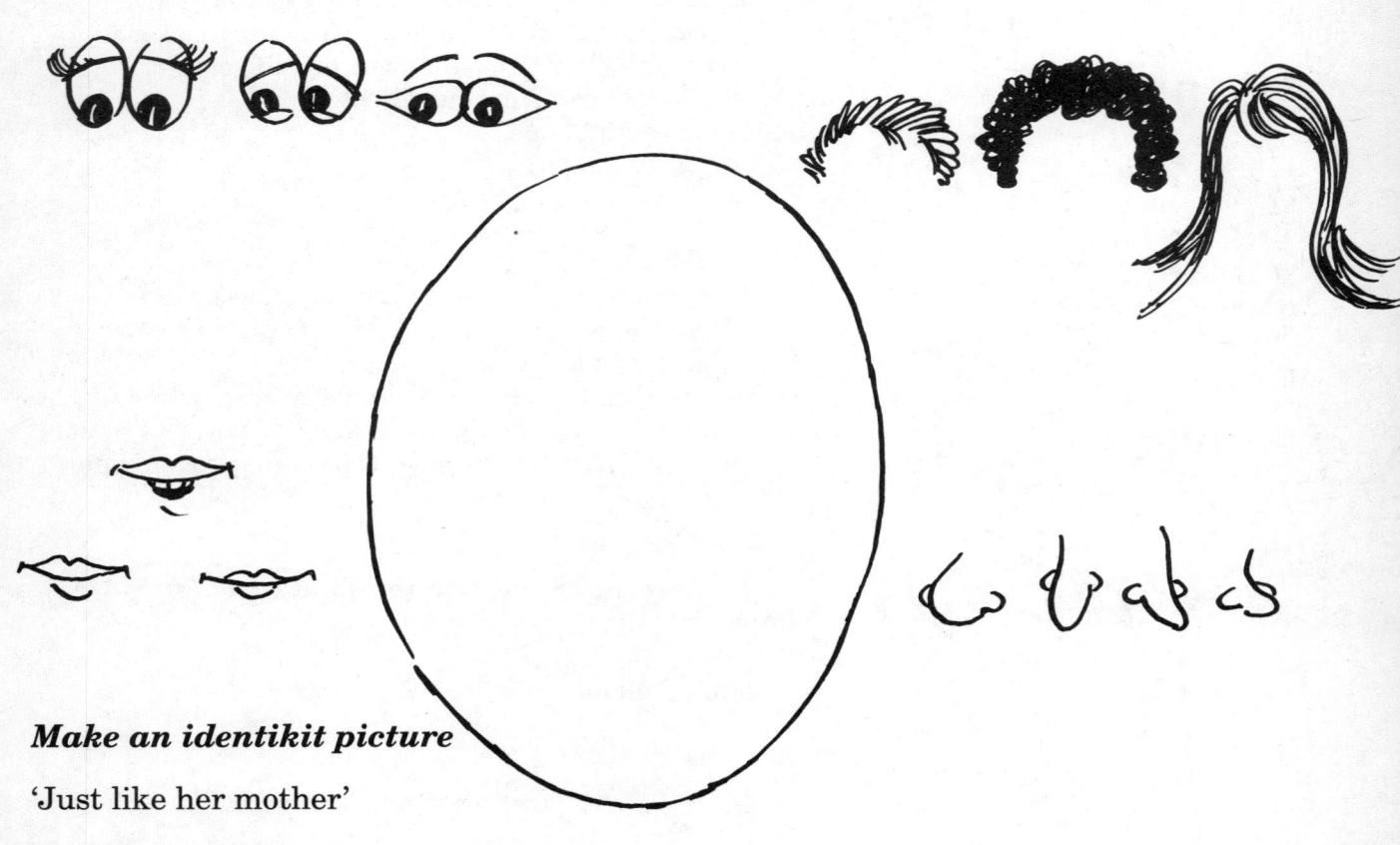

Make an identikit picture

'Just like her mother'

'Like father, like son'

Who do you most look like in your family?

32

Thoughts for adults

'Just like your mother'. 'It's from your side of the family'. 'Your father will never be dead while you're alive', are phrases which not only give us an indication of how others see us, they also remind us of our own roots and where we come from. It's often not until later in life that we begin to see the truth in what people are saying and then only with hindsight after some key event.

The resurrection experiences of the disciples gave them a much greater insight into the significance of Jesus' life and all that he had said and done. They recalled Jesus saying: 'To have seen me is to have seen the Father'; and 'I am the Father and the Father is in me'.

They had struggled to understand Jesus and now it was clear: Jesus is God revealed to us. Jesus makes clear what God is like. This revelation not only makes clear who God is and who Jesus is, it makes us realise our own importance too. God became a person like us; God is very close to us.

A thought from Scripture: John 14:9-13.

With the children

- Watch them. Ask yourself who are they most like?
- Help them to see family resemblances.
- Help them to see what they have in common with other people and what is unique to them..

Say a prayer together:

God our Father,
Thank you for sending your Son Jesus
to live with us.
We now know what you are like!
We often wondered.

Thank you for giving us Jesus,
a person just like us,
because he helps us to see that we are special!
Help us to remember that all people are precious.
Amen.

Who else are you like in your family?

I'm as kind as...

I'm as happy go lucky as...

I'm as cool as...

I'm as clever as...

I'm as generous as...

I'm as lively as...

I'm as funny as...

I'm good at...

just like...

The two people most alike in our family are

....

and ....

People often say I am just like...

Celebrating Easter – Jesus is with us

The new term had begun and Emma was thrilled to know that Amina would be coming to her school. They were both up very early. Amina put on her best clothes, the ones she had been given for Id-ul-fitr.

When they arrived the Headteacher asked Emma to show Amina where to hang her coat and then take her to class. The Headteacher and class teacher welcomed Amina and made a place for her by Emma. For the rest of the morning Emma proudly showed Amina where everything was kept.

At playtime lots of children gathered around them, they wanted to know all about Amina. They all played a game together. In the game Emma and Amina were partners.

After lunch while they were playing in the yard, some older children came over to tease them. Emma quickly told the dinner lady who chased them away.

They stayed close together all day, Amina never once got lost. On the way home Amina turned to Emma and said, "I'm glad I have you for a friend."

People who make life better for me

I'm always glad when………. is at home.

I love to be with ……….

My best friend is……….

When I go on a message at school, I'm always glad to have………. with me.

I like to walk home with……….

Thoughts for adults

Jesus has risen from the dead and is with us, that's the message of Easter.

The disciples became conscious and aware of the presence of Jesus in the most ordinary of situations, by the lakeside, cooking, at the meal table, in the hired room as well as in the garden. He had not left them, they knew it and rejoiced.

He has not left us, he is present with us too in the most ordinary of situations, though like the disciples on their way to Emmaus, we don't always notice that he is in our company. Like them we come to recognise him in the breaking of bread. He comes to us and is present with us in the many people who care for us and help us out each day. Some of them we live with, others we meet by chance.

*(Id-ul-fitr celebrates the end of Ramadan, the Muslim season of self-denial. It is celebrated by giving to charities, present-giving to family and friends, and new clothes.)

A thought from Scripture: John 20:29.

With the children

- Tell them about a time when someone helped you out, someone who you thanked God for.
- Help them to name all the people who care for and look after them.
- Help them with the activity.

At prayer time

Each think of one person who has helped you today.
Picture them again in your mind's eye.
When someone helps us we are really being helped by Jesus even though they don't look like or sound like him. When we help others, it's Jesus who gives us the idea. It's very hard to believe because we can't see him!

Listen to the words of Jesus:
"Jesus said to his disciples,
"You know that I am alive
because you can see me.
May God bless all those people
who will not be able to see me
but will still believe in me."
(Or use the prayer on p. 33.)

Rescued!

Once, when I was stuck at
.... my ....
came to help me.

Once, when I was really
frightened...............
rescued me.

Once, when I was lonely
with no one for company
....
came to play with me.

....
is always coming to the
rescue of our family.

Warmer Weather

"We've got my paddling pool out!" announced Tommy at Emma's door.

The weather had suddenly turned much warmer taking everyone by surprise. Some people were already dressed in summer clothes, whilst others kept their coats on, sure that at any moment the weather would turn much colder.

Neil and Louise ran over to see Tommy's pool. Emma ran to the cupboard where her clothes were kept.

"What on earth are you doing?" called mum. "Looking for my swimming costume. "Every one's playing in Tommy's pool."

Emma found her costume, and as quick as a flash had it on. "Take it off, it doesn't fit you. You've grown out of it."

Mum was right, it didn't fit, but Emma was determined to play in the pool. "It's alright!" and grabbing a towel she ran to Tommy's.

Some of the neighbours had gathered to watch the children play. "Don't get too used to it," said Mrs Ward, "this weather won't last. It's spring not summer. Helen isn't getting in." With that Helen, who had been pleading with her mum to let her join in, ran home and slammed the door in temper.

"Well, I love it!" said Tommy's mum, sitting on the doorstep wearing her suntop. "Don't cast a clout till May is out," added Mrs Kelly.

A few nights later there was a terrible thunderstom. Emma was so frightened she climbed into mum's bed.

"Is God angry?" she asked. "No," mum explained.

The next day it was as cold as ever, there was even talk of snow.

Thoughts for adults

Each spring there are a few days of warmer weather taking everyone by surprise. No sooner have we adjusted to it, there's a thunderstorm and the cool weather returns. Our unpredictable weather affects our lives and our moods and, sometimes, our images of God. Yet all types of weather are needed. All of them have their part to play, even the thunderstorms.

We in our turn are part of creation and our behaviour affects the rest of creation. Perhaps even the weather patterns are changing because of the activities of the human race. The planet earth is good, but vulnerable to our abuse.

God, as Creator of everything, invites us to live in harmony with all creation and to care for it. The new life given us through the death and the resurrection of Jesus will include the whole of creation; God the Father, who loves all created things will bring all things to fulfilment in Him.

A thought from Scripture: Psalm 95:4-5 or Ephesians 1: 3-10.

With the children

- Encourage them to notice the weather, make weather charts. Children often have very stereotyped ideas about the weather, convinced, for example, that it snows every Christmas Day, that every summer is very hot and that particular days of the week have regular weather patterns.
- Talk about fears, thunderstorms. Try to avoid using false imagery, for example, 'angels moving furniture' or 'God stamping his feet'. It can be far more frightening than the truth, and may give a false image of God.
- Help them to see that wet, windy weather, though unpleasant, is life-giving. Try planting seeds outdoors. Ask the children to take care of them.

A prayer to say

Father,
you give us rain, wind, sun snow, fog
and weather of all kinds,
often on a day we don't want it.
Help us to trust you,
to thank you
and to enjoy your gift of weather,
whatever the weather!   Amen.

Weather lore

Wind is..................

Foggy weather can be

....

A traditional rhyme
Whether the weather be fine
Whether the weather be not
Whether the weather be cold
Whether the weather be hot
We'll weather the weather
Whatever the weather
Whether we like it or not!

The rain makes me feel

....

When it's hot I...............

Thunderstorms...............

Snow is........................

May Day – Bank Holiday

There was a poster outside Mr Cohen's shop advertising a gala to be held on the playing fields. Helen noticed the children looking at it. She ran over to them. "I'm in the dancing competition, I hope I win."

"My mum is in the keep fit display," said Jim and he made all the children laugh by showing them what his mum did. Louise, still looking at the picture noticed the dog show.

"Let's take the Kelly's dog, we might win," she told the others.

"Not likely!" said Tommy. "Anyway I'm in the go-cart race."

"Forget it all," said Denis Kelly coming out of Mr Cohen's shop, "It's been cancelled, the field is not safe."

When Mrs Kelly heard the news she was disappointed too.

"We'll have our own," she announced, "without competitions, they only lead to arguments and disappointments. Helen you can dance, Tommy you can show us your go-cart, Jim we'd love to see your mum's keep fit display. Everyone can join in."

Nearly everyone in the road did join in, making tea, showing pets, it was a great laugh. Even Mr Carrick who never left his house, came out to have a look.

When it was nearly over one of the neighbours complained, saying that they were making a show of the road.

"We've never been so happy and proud to live here," said the adults. "Yeah," cheered the children. Then they all went home.

"I'm lost"

A card game that needs other people's help.

One: The dealer spreads a whole pack of cards face down on a table

Two: The dealer turns one card over (for example, 3 of Hearts) and shouts 'I'm lost!' Then the other players must turn over the other cards one at a time, taking turns to find the 3s of Diamonds, Clubs and Spades.

Three: As each card is found they are given to the dealer who then turns all the other cards face down again.

Four: The dealer turns another card over and shouts 'I'm lost'... and so on until the dealer has all the cards together again. When the pack is complete the game ends

Five: Time how long it takes from the first upturned card till the pack is complete. What's your fastest score?

Thoughts for adults

Another holiday in the Easter Season. What a blessing! What a gift! Our best response is to go out and enjoy it in the company of others.

Jesus came so that we might have life and life to the full! Life to the full is all that you can imagine and dream it to be and more. Though to achieve this means a more co-operative than competitive approach. We don't achieve life to the full at the expense of others.

A thought from Scripture: Acts 4: 32-35.

With the children

- Find a way of enjoying God's creation (inexpensively).
- Invite other people into your company.
- Try the card game. It is based on co-operation rather than competition.
- Spend time together enjoying one another's company.

At prayer time

Think back over the day,
Thank you God for today.
The best parts were...
The worst part was...
I will never forget...
If I could live today again tomorrow I would...
I'm sorry that...
God bless all the people who I met today, especially...

It's still Easter

Emma went as usual to Mrs Kelly's after school. This evening some of the other children were there too. They were talking about Easter eggs.

"I have six Easter eggs left," announced Tommy.

"I've two," said Jim.

"So, have I," added Helen. "I've got one with chocolates and one without."

"I've only one," said Emma.

Neil couldn't believe it. He'd long since eaten all of his. He began to wonder if Louise had any left. He looked over to her. "Yes, I've still got one," she grinned.

That made it worse. He knew she would tease him with every mouthful!

"Easter has been over for ages, you should have eaten all your eggs by now!" he shouted to everyone.

Tom Kelly overheard Neil and began to laugh at him which made Neil really angry.

Mrs Kelly came in to see what was the matter.

"When does Easter finish?" asked Helen.

"Well Pentecost Sunday, I suppose, but it really goes on forever."

"Forever?" asked the children.

"Easter isn't just about the day or a few weeks that we celebrate. It's about knowing that no matter how bad things are, wonderful things, unbelieveable things can happen. They don't just happen at Easter either, they can happen anytime in the year. There's lots of good times ahead."

Neil thought about the best thing that could happen to him; after a while he smiled, saying, "I don't mind about the eggs, they don't matter so much."

The best!

What's the *best* that can happen to you?

How many extra Easter eggs can you find in this picture?

Thoughts for adults

Life isn't easy. A constant barrage of everyday worries and concerns with occasional disasters can darken our view of life. It's easy to feel powerless and face every situation imagining that the worst possible outcome is inevitable.

Easter calls us to rise above such a pessimistic approach. The resurrection gives us confidence that even our wildest dreams can come true! The unimaginable and the unbelieveable are really possible. The Easter moment transforms our lives and we become Easter People, confident in God and in the power of good. Confident that God is always faithful to his promises, we work for a better world, a world in which everyone enjoys a life of dignity.

A thought from Scripture: 1 Peter: 1:3-9.

With the children

- Share one of your clearest dreams and listen to their's.
- Share a time when one of your dreams came true.
- Share a hope, a dream for the world, the kind of world you would like them to inherit.
- Help them with the activity.

At prayer time

Light the Easter candle, or whatever light you pray near. Put out of your mind any worries (give them to Jesus to look after). Put into your mind the good moments of the day.

Jesus, Easter has taught us
that great things can happen,
dreams do come true.
Glory be to God!

Now we are Easter People
we will look forward to the future
we'll be hopeful, we won't worry.
Glory be to God!

Help us not to give up
hope when things are difficult.
Help us to always remember
that for you all is possible.
Glory be to God!

Ascension – Saying Goodbye

"If you're playing out keep clean and be back here by three o'clock," said auntie Joan, "and don't go too far!"

"Why?" everyone chorused.

"You'll see and find out soon enough," said mum.

Louise and Neil looked at each other and then with Emma went out to play. They enjoyed playing out so much that they didn't notice the time until suddenly Tommy announced that he was going in to watch TV.

"It must be well past three," shouted Louise, "we're in trouble." They ran back home as fast as they could. As they turned the corner they saw mum and Auntie Joan waiting for them. Running so fast they didn't notice Uncle Alex at first but as soon as they did they knew what it meant.

"Dad!" called Neil.

"Hi!" shouted Uncle Alex and he gave them all a big hug. "Get in the car, we're going home." There were lots of 'goodbyes' and promises to 'phone.

Emma watched them drive off. She felt sad and lonely. She knew they might go home sometime, but why now. As she and mum went back into the house it seemed different, very different. "There's no point in cooking a big meal. Put the TV on Emma, it's too quiet here."

Turning on the TV Emma asked, "When will we see them again?"

"Don't worry, we'll keep in touch," said mum.

Keep count!

How many people are you in touch with this week?

Put a • for each 'phone call, letter or message.

How many times did the phone ring or someone use the phone in your house?

How many letters of any kind came in and out of your house?

How many messages were given in your house? e.g. Tea's ready!

Another way to keep count is by tally marks, a downward stroke instead of a dot. The 5th, 10th, 15th, 20th, 25th... stroke goes across. This way it is easy to count. e.g.

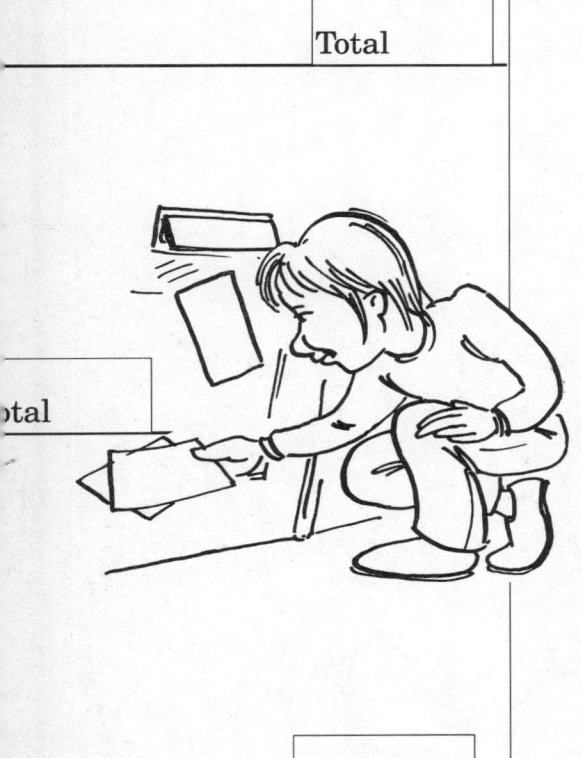

1	2	3	4	5
/	//	///	////	####
6	7	8	9	10
#### /	#### //	#### ///	#### ////	#### ####

Thoughts for adults

There are all sorts of moments in our lives when we know that we must let go and move on: growing up, getting married, changing job, moving house, retirement. However necessary, parting can be difficult. For a while we can feel a 'draught'. We need time to accept new circumstances. In the period of readjustment we learn to do things differently. We find other ways of keeping contact, keeping in touch. Though sometimes painful, partings can be full of great potential too. We can discover and develop strengths and resources within ourselves previously unnoticed.

Jesus' farewell was one of promise and potential. When the time came for him to return to his Father, he promised the disciples that he would not leave them alone, he promised to send the Spirit. The Feast of the Ascension celebrates this promise. It celebrates the last time the disciples saw Jesus and it celebrates their new relationship with Him.

A thought from Scripture: John 16:5-15.

With the children

- Get in touch with a friend or relative you miss.
- Talk over ways of keeping in touch.
- Look at family photos. How do they keep you in touch?

At prayer time

Close your eyes.
Pretend you are there with the disciples, try hard to imagine what the place would look like.
What would you like to say to Jesus?
(Keep it a secret just for you and Jesus.)
What do you think he would say to you?
(Listen to him and keep it a secret too).
If a family bereavement has come up in discussion:
God our Father,
We pray for..... who have died, but are living with you now, so we know they're happy.
Give them our love, we miss them,
but we look forward to the day
when we shall be with them and you in heaven. Amen.

Pentecost – Birthday of the Church

"For goodness sake play out!" shouted mum.

"I've no one to play with now Louise and Neil have gone home. I don't like playing out without them," moaned Emma, pulling a face more miserable than ever. Mum saw it. "That's it! Bed! It's no use moping around here. Bed, until you've changed your face."

Emma stamped up to her room. She hated her bedroom on summer evenings. It took her ages to get to sleep at night. The street was always so noisy. It was especially noisy this evening. She went over to the window to see what was going on. Looking outside she noticed four children new to the street. 'Where have they come from?' she wondered and wondered and wondered. Suddenly she felt brave and as keen to play out as when she had had Lousie and Neil for company. She tumbled down the stairs shouting, "Can I play out, mum?"

Out in the street she met the children, Joe, Anna, Cathy and Christopher. They had just moved into the house next door to Mr Carrick. "Do you live here?" they asked. "Who else lives here? What's it like?"

"It's great!" Then Emma told them all about the Kellys, the Roaches, the Wards, the Askaris, the Greenwoods, Mr Carrick and even Mr Cohen's shop. She told them about the wonderful things these people did and the wonderful times they had together, the street carnival and the days out. As she spoke she realised how clever and special these really were. "It's really great here and you can join in everything, everything!"

Mum watched and smiled, "They might have a few ideas too!"

Happy Birthday

Light the candles that are part of your parish life. Write in the candles what happens in your parish. You may need more candles. Ask the people in your parish for help.

Write in your parish's name. On the cherries and chocolate buttons collect the autographs of all the people who do good things in your parish.

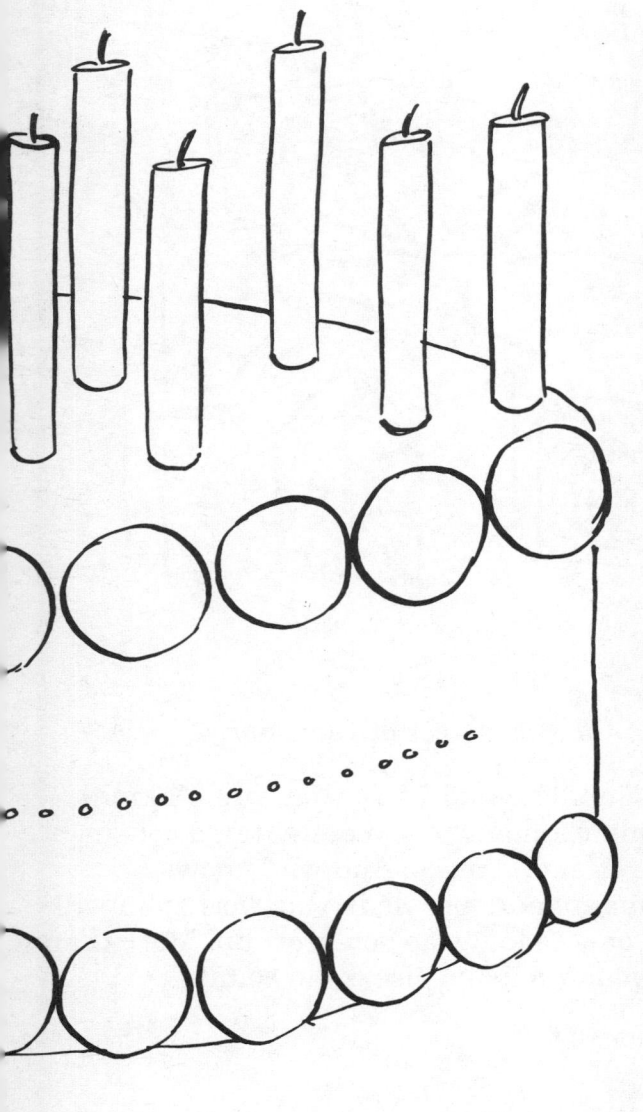

Thoughts for adults

Kindness, tolerance, sense of justice, patience, humour, sensitivity, dedication, perseverance, cheerfulness, willingness to take a risk, wisdom, thoughtfulness, sense of adventure, respect for others, love of people, love of the environment and animals, being loving and lovable, ingenuity; the list of gifts given to us are endless. They are a sign to us of the presence of God the Holy Spirit in our world. Our ability to recognise them as such is a further gift, a gift of faith.

And yet the presence of the Spirit at Pentecost is no ordinary event. It breaks through all laws of nature as we understand them. The wind, the fire, the transformed disciples, all speak powerfully of the presence of the Spirit. The Spirit is a gift, given to us continuously and because of the Spirit we and the world in which we live can be transformed.

A thought from Scripture: 1 Corinthians 12: 4-11.

With the children

- Tell one another about the qualities which are your special gifts as individuals and members of a family.
- Make a birthday cake. On the cake put a candle for each member of your family. Add a few candles to represent the people you know in your parish. As you blow out the candles, ask for God's blessing on all of you. Maybe sing 'Happy Birthday to you...'(*insert the parish name*)

At prayer time

Light your candles:

Dear Father,
make us brave enough
to believe that we are gifted.
Make us brave enough
to use our gifts.
Give us the courage to be like your Son, Jesus.
We ask this as good friends of his. Amen.

Trinity Sunday

Emma woke up and then realised 'It's my birthday!' Quick as a flash she was out of bed, into mum's room to wake her up, and downstairs to open her cards.

They were scattered on the floor by the door. Emma sat next to them opening each one as fast as she could. She read the titles out aloud.

"For my Daughter..... from Mum.

A Birthday Wish for My Friend... from Anna.

A Special Niece... from Auntie Joan.

To a Special Girl on her Birthday... from Mrs Kelly

Happy Birthday Cousin... from Louise and Neil."

There were lots more, some with badges too. She counted them and there were eleven in all.

"Look! They say, cousin, friend, daughter, special girl – that's me! They're all about me. I've eleven cards! I know eleven people."

"Some of these cards have more than one name on," said mum, getting the breakfast ready.

Emma began to count again, "Twenty-three! I know twenty-three people."

"You know even more. Not everyone you know will send you a card. Think of the people at school, the others in our street, the people you see on the way to school..."

"Stop! I can't count that many."

Mum laughed. "Yes, they will all know my Emma who is a daughter, a cousin, a friend, a niece. And who knows how many more people in this world you will come to know as you grow up. More than you or anyone else could count."

Make a list of all the people you know

Grandparents
Parents
Brothers
Sisters
Cousins
Friends
Uncles
Aunties
Neighbours
Acquaintances

People you would like to get to know

How many altogether?
....

Which parts of this list might change?

Thoughts for adults

We've probably more relationships than we can recall or count. Some grow and develop, others are passing. Whatever the kind, each affects us in a different way. Our relationships too, do not begin and end with those we meet. There are the many people we'll never meet who are very much affected by the lives we lead.

For most of us, our first relationships are with our parents. 'Mum', 'Dad' may be the first words we speak as children, though it can take all sorts of experiences before we begin to understand what such words mean. It can take a lifetime to grow into the relationship; a lifetime to really say 'Mum', 'Dad'.

The life of God is a life of love given and received between Father, Son and Holy Spirit. The Spirit continues to draw each of us into relationship with the Father and the Son, with each other, with people we know and do not know and with the world in which we live. The Spirit, the Father and the Son empower and call us to reach out beyond ourselves.

A thought from Scripture: Matthew 19:20 or Romans 8: 14-17.

With the children

- Next time there is a birthday, look at all the cards and notice the different types of relationships.
- Talk over new and old relationships: how they change.
- Encourage the children to reach out, to make new friends.
- If they are older (9 years or so upwards), talk about the responsibility various relationships bring.
- Encourage them to have respect for the natural world, keep a pet, try some gardening etc.

A prayer to say

Glory be to the Father and to the Son and to the Holy Spirit,
As it was in the beginning, is now and ever shall be. Amen.

God, we know so many people,
more and more each day.
Help us to be kind to those we meet,
to take care of what we say.
Help us not to spoil the world for others who live in it
and for the peole who are yet to live here,
for they and the world in which we all live
are your gift to us. Amen.

What was in the Easter eggs?

No. 1 Three small eggs
No. 2 A bag of sweets and a puzzle
No. 3 Toffee
No. 4 Under the egg is £2.00
No. 5 Nothing
No. 6 Nothing, the extra chocolates were on top.
No. 7 Under the egg, inside the box a £5.00 note.
No. 8 Nothing
No. 9 Creme icing.

Surprised? The outside doesn't tell us very much.   It's the same with people. How we look on the outside has nothing to do with what we're really like on the inside. What's special about you, inside?

Collins Liturgical Publications
77 - 85 Fulham Palace Road,
Hammersmith, London W6 8JB

Collins Dove
PO Private Bag 200, Burwood,
Victoria 3125, Australia

Collins Liturgical New Zealand
PO Box 1, Auckland

ISBN 0 00 599 266 4

First published 1991
© 1991 Department for Catholic Education and Formation
Bishops' Conference of England and Wales

Nihil obstat: Fr. Anton Cowan, *censor*
Imprimatur Rt. Rev. John Crowley, V.G.
Westminster, 4th October, 1990

The Nihil obstat and Imprimatur are a declaration that a book or pamphlet is considered to be free from doctrinal or moral error. It is not implied that those who have granted the Nihil obstat or Imprimatur agree with the contents, opinions or statements expressed.

Designed by Malcolm Harvey Young
Ilustrated by Lorraine White
Manufactured in Great Britain by Bell & Bain Ltd, Glasgow